D0602035

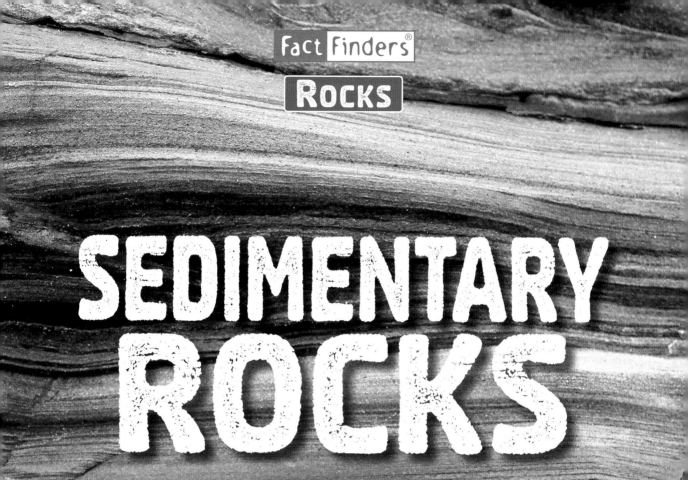

Fact Finders®

Rocks

SEDIMENTARY ROCKS

by Ava Sawyer

CAPSTONE PRESS
a capstone imprint

Fact Finders Books are published by Capstone Press,
1710 Roe Crest Drive, North Mankato, Minnesota 56003
www.mycapstone.com

Copyright © 2019 by Capstone Press, a Capstone imprint. All rights
reserved. No part of this publication may be reproduced in whole or
in part, or stored in a retrieval system, or transmitted in any form or
by any means, electronic, mechanical, photocopying, recording,
or otherwise, without written permission of the publisher.

Library of Congress Cataloging-in-Publication Data
Names: Sawyer, Ava, author.
Title: Sedimentary rocks / by Ava Sawyer.
Description: North Mankato, Minnesota : Capstone Press, [2018] |
    Series: Fact finders. Rocks | Audience: Ages 8–10. | Includes index.
Identifiers: LCCN 2017059335 (print) | LCCN 2018005718 (ebook)
    | ISBN 9781543527193 (ebook PDF) | ISBN 9781543527032
    (library binding) | ISBN 9781543527117 (paperback)
Subjects: LCSH: Sedimentary rocks—Juvenile literature. |
    Petrology—Juvenile literature.
Classification: LCC QE471 (ebook) | LCC QE471 .S37325 2018
    (print) | DDC 552/.5—dc23
LC record available at https://lccn.loc.gov/2017059335

Editorial Credits
Editor: Nikki Potts
Designer: Sarah Bennett
Media Researcher: Jo Miller
Production Specialist: Laura Manthe

Image Credits
Dreamstime: Volgariver, cover; NASA: Provided by the SeaWiFS
Project, NASA/Goddard Space Flight Center, and ORBIMAGE,
15; Science Source: Spencer Sutton, 25; Shutterstock: abutyrin,
29, Aleksei Kornev, 20, Alexlukin, 22 (top), Alison Hancock, 26
(right), Been there YB, 27, Breck P. Kent, 18, Dave Porter, 23, Doug
Lemke, 2-3, Elzbieta Sekowska, 14, Ethan Daniels, 11, EyeTravel,
13, Fokin Oleg, 22 (bottom), Imfoto, 5, Jausa, 22 (middle top), Jiri
Prochazka, 10, KarenHBlack, 24, marekuliasz, 22 (middle bottom),
Mark Godden, 6, Rocket Photos, 8-9, Rudmer Zwerver, 29 (top),
Sergei Afanasev, 4, sonsam, 17 (bottom), Sopotnicki, 16, studioloco,
28, tororo reaction, 19, Tyler Boyes, 17 (top), umat34, 21, Vladislav
Gajic, 7, xshot, 26 (left)

Design Elements
Shutterstock: Alted Studio, SAPhotog

Printed in the United States of America.
PA021

TABLE OF CONTENTS

Photo: Dead Horse Point State Park near Canyonlands National Park, Utah

CHAPTER 1
WHAT ARE SEDIMENTARY ROCKS?

Beaches are covered with grains of sand. Rivers are colored with bits of mud. Sand and mud do not look anything like a rock. However, they are some of the basic materials that make up sedimentary rock.

Sedimentary rocks are made from particles of rock, soil, and other materials. These particles are commonly known as sediment. The particles come in many sizes. Some particles are as large as gravel. Other particles are as small as dust. From the highest mountain to the deepest ocean floor, sedimentary rocks form only under conditions that exist on Earth's surface.

The Kura and Aragvi rivers merge near Mtskheta in the country of Georgia.

Some sediment includes minerals, and other sediment includes fossils. Pieces of sediment form rocks when they are forced together by pressure. Some are cemented together by minerals carried in groundwater.

MINERALS

A mineral is a solid, nonliving material found only in nature. Minerals are made up of microscopic atoms that are organized into crystals. These crystals have a three-dimensional structure, such as a cube or pyramid. Graphite is one of the softest minerals. A diamond is one of the hardest. Both are made of only carbon atoms. The structure of their crystals is what gives them different properties.

About 3,000 kinds of minerals serve as the building blocks of all rocks found on Earth. Some minerals, such as salt and graphite, are common and easy to find. Others, such as diamonds and gold, are very rare.

uncut diamonds

fossil—remains of an ancient plant or animal that have hardened into rock; also the preserved tracks or outline of an ancient organism

crystal—a solid substance having a regular pattern of many flat surfaces

The presence of fossils in sedimentary rocks makes this type of rock **unique**. The two other types of rocks on Earth are metamorphic rocks and igneous rocks. Due to how these types of rocks are formed, they do not contain fossils.

Some sedimentary rocks have just a few fossils in them. Others are made almost entirely of fossils. For example, limestone is made up of coral and crushed seashells. Coal is formed from the remains of prehistoric plants buried in sediment. Over millions of years, these plant remains turned into a burnable rock.

A large ammonite fossil is preserved in a piece of limestone.

FOSSIL FUELS

Fossil fuels are nonrenewable resources that will either run out or take thousands of years to replace. Coal, oil, and natural gas are some of the most well-known fossil fuels. We rely on fossil fuels as an energy source.

Fossil fuels come from the remains of plants that lived millions of years ago. Much of Earth was covered in swamps during this time. When a plant or animal died, it sank and became buried. Over time, layers of material formed over the remains, creating great pressure. High temperatures and pressure caused the remains to turn to rock.

Today these fossil fuels are mined and extracted from deep within Earth. Coal, oil, and natural gas can be burned or refined and then used as an energy source. While there are large amounts of some fossil fuels, people burn through them quickly. At the current rate of use, scientists estimate the world's reserves will last 40 to 70 more years.

Large areas of land are dug up to remove coal.

unique—one of a kind

fossil fuel—natural fuel formed from the remains of plants and animals; coal, oil, and natural gas are fossil fuels

extract—to remove

reserve—something stored or kept available for future use or need

CHAPTER 2

How Sedimentary Rocks Form

Sedimentary rocks form in many ways. However, all of those ways require pressure to combine the loose pieces of sediment into a sedimentary rock.

The basic process of creating a sedimentary rock begins with a layer of sand, gravel, fossils, and other particles. Those particles are dropped onto the ground by moving water, wind, or glaciers. Over time, more sediment gets piled onto the original sediment. New layers form on top of the old layers. Tiny particles of sand and soil fill in the gaps between the larger particles.

With each new layer of sediment, more weight pushes down on the layers below. As more layers of sediment are added, the pressure on the lower layers increases. The rocks and soil in the lower layers are squeezed together. When water is present, some of the particles are dissolved. They then turn into a type of cement that glues the other sediments together. When the water eventually evaporates, a solid layer of sedimentary rock is left behind.

The formation of sedimentary rock is not a quick process. It can take thousands of years or longer for sedimentary rocks to form naturally.

view of the Grand Canyon from
Bright Angel Point on the North Rim

CHAPTER 3

MOVING SEDIMENT

Rocks on Earth are broken up by weathering and erosion. Wind, water, and other forces break up and move rocks. For example, when waves crash on the shore, they break up rocks on the shoreline. These rocks eventually turn into tiny particles of sand. The sediment can then be swept away to a new location by moving water, wind, and glaciers through erosion. There are two types of weathering—physical and chemical.

PHYSICAL WEATHERING

Physical weathering breaks rocks into smaller pieces, such as boulders, pebbles, and granules. The smallest pieces created by this type of weathering are sand and silt. Snow, sleet, and hail tear away at granite mountaintops. Water seeps into cracks in a rock, freezes, expands, and breaks the rock. These are examples of physical weathering. During this process, the chemical makeup of the rock does not change. The rock material stays the same.

weathering—breaking down of solid rock into smaller and smaller pieces by wind, water, glaciers, or plant roots

erosion—wearing away of rock or soil by wind, water, or ice

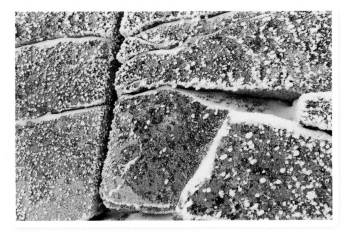

Water creates breaks in rocks as it freezes and expands.

Limestone islands in Indonesia are created by physical and chemical weathering.

CHEMICAL WEATHERING

During the chemical weathering process, the minerals, or chemical components, of the rock change. For example, when water drips on or over rocks, some of its minerals dissolve in the water. The rock's chemical makeup changes and creates something new. In limestone, for example, the oxygen in water combines with feldspar and other minerals. The results are new minerals that make up clay.

EROSION

Water, wind, and glaciers are all types of erosion. Sources of moving water include rivers and streams. The water picks up and carries sediment downstream. Tiny particles of soil in the water will turn the water into the same color as the soil. That is why some rivers or streams look brown, gray, or red. The water in those rivers and streams is moving colored sediment.

If the water in a river or stream is moving fast, then it will be able to carry sand, gravel, and other sediment. Water that is moving really fast can even carry boulders. The sand, gravel, and other sediment come from either the edges of the river or from the riverbed.

As the water slows down, it loses energy and strength. The moving water can no longer carry all of the particles. When this happens, the particles are left behind. The larger particles are deposited, or dropped, first. By the time the water from a river or stream reaches a sea or lake, the water is usually moving very slowly. That is when the very fine, lighter particles of sand and soil are deposited.

FACT

The Mississippi River **Delta** Basin is made up of about 521,000 acres (210,841 hectares) of land. Here, the Mississippi River deposits sediment at an average of 470,000 cubic feet (13,309 cubic meters) per second into the Gulf of Mexico.

delta—an area of land shaped like a triangle where a river enters a sea or ocean

Wind also carries sediment. Wind picks up loose soil, sand, or other particles from the earth and blows them around. The particles then land in another place, whether it is just a few feet or many miles away from the original location.

Glaciers also move sediment from one place to another. These big sheets of ice are very powerful. They can easily move large boulders. When the boulders slide across the land, they break other rocks into smaller pieces. This sediment either stays in place or is also moved by the glacier.

Jbel Saghro mountains in Morocco

GREAT LAKES

The Great Lakes system is one of the youngest geographical features in North America. It formed about 12,000 years ago, at the end of the most recent Ice Age. During the Ice Age, the planet's climate grew much colder. Huge, moving sheets of ice called glaciers crept southward. As the heavy glaciers moved, they carried rocks and dirt with them, reforming the land as they went. By about 20,000 years ago, much of North America was covered in the giant Laurentide ice sheet.

About 12,000 years ago, the Ice Age ended. The planet's climate warmed. The glaciers retreated northward. They continued to reshape the land as they moved. In many places, the glaciers moved only the top layer of rock. The solid bedrock beneath resisted erosion. But the area where the Great Lakes formed was covered in thick layers of soft sedimentary rocks such as sandstone and shale. As the glaciers retreated, they cut into this soft rock, gouging out deep basins.

As the ice sheet melted, it left behind massive amounts of meltwater. This water collected in the deep basins it had carved out, forming the Great Lakes.

The five Great Lakes are Lake Erie, Lake Michigan, Lake Superior, Lake Huron, and Lake Ontario.

CHAPTER 4

IDENTIFYING SEDIMENTARY ROCKS

Sedimentary rocks are identified using a variety of characteristics. Sedimentary rocks do not usually have a shiny appearance. They are typically easier to break than either igneous or metamorphic rocks. If a rock has a fossil in it, then it is a sedimentary rock. But not all sedimentary rocks contain fossils.

Sedimentary rocks form in various ways. How rocks form is one way geologists classify sedimentary rocks.

A sign at Yosemite National Park in California warns visitors to watch for falling rocks.

CLASTIC ROCK

breccia

Geologists use the term *clastic* for sedimentary rocks that form from physical or chemical weathering. Clastics begin with physical weathering. For example, sedimentary rocks first break off from a mountain. These big chunks with sharp angles are call **breccias**. As breccias move down the mountainside, they bump together. The bumping begins to round the rocks' edges. As the rocks move downhill, they continue to be smoothed and rounded by wind or water. They eventually form **conglomerates**. The conglomerates grind into sand or silt. These small pieces are carried down the mountain quickly by wind and water. The larger pieces are left behind.

conglomerate

The small pieces of sand can also undergo chemical weathering. Atoms in the sand can combine in new ways with atoms in the water and atmosphere. This results in clay. The fine particles that make up clay are an important part in forming soil.

Geologists also classify sedimentary rock based on its size. The farther a piece of rock travels from its source, the smaller it will be. For example, gravel is made of bigger pieces such as breccias and conglomerates. Shale is made of tiny particles of clay.

geologist—someone who studies minerals, rocks, and soil
breccia—sedimentary rock formed from jagged pieces of rock cemented together
conglomerate—sedimentary rock formed from small, rounded chunks cemented together

CARBONATE ROCK

Minerals that dissolve in water and form new minerals create chemical sedimentary rocks called carbonates. Limestone is one of the best-known chemical sedimentary rocks. The main mineral in limestone is calcite. Limestone can form when calcite is removed from water. Calcite can be removed in two ways.

When warm salt water evaporates, layers of the hard, rock-forming mineral calcite are deposited. Calcite from water pouring out of mineral springs often hardens into the shape of giant steps. This type of rock is called travertine. Water dripping inside a cave evaporates to make limestone in icicle-like shapes called **stalactites** and **stalagmites**.

Stalactites and stalagmites grow in a cave in Luray, Virginia.

The second way calcite is removed is with the help of sea creatures. They take in calcite from the water and use it to make shells. When the creatures die, their shells fall to the seafloor. The current and waves grind the shells into tiny pieces of sediment. Over time, the calcite sediment hardens into limestone rock.

FACT

Australia's Great Barrier Reef and other coral reefs are made of limestone formed from the calcite shells of dead coral animals.

coral reefs

stalactite—a rock formation that hangs from the ceiling of a cave and is formed by dripping water

stalagmite—a rock formation that grows from the floor of a cave; it is formed when water drips onto the cave floor and leaves minerals behind

OTHER TYPES OF SEDIMENTARY ROCKS

A few of the most well-known sedimentary rocks are sandstone, gritstone, mudstone, and claystone. Sandstone is just what it sounds like. It is millions of grains of loose sand that have been hardened into stone. Sandstone has a rough texture and feels like sandpaper. The grains of sand in sandstone are rounded and are made mainly of the mineral quartz. Sandstone can come in many different colors. In the southwestern United States sandstone is most often a bright orange-red color.

FACT

Quartz is made of silicon and oxygen. It is the most abundant mineral found in the continental crust—Earth's outer layer. Quartz is also commonly found in sandy beaches.

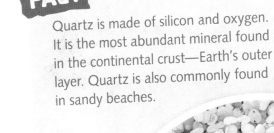

Bryce Canyon National Park in Utah

Gritstone is similar to sandstone. It is made in the same way with the same types of materials. However, the sand grains are much larger in this stone and are not rounded. This makes the texture of gritstone feel much rougher than the texture of sandstone.

Mudstone is formed when great pressure is added to mud in a riverbed or seabed. The grains in this stone are extremely small. You cannot see them with a magnifying glass or a microscope. This stone can be black, green, gray, or red in color. Mudstone is also brittle, which means it can break easily.

Just like mudstone, claystone has very small grains that cannot be seen with a magnifying glass or microscope. When claystone gets wet, it is soft and easy to break. It is also a slippery rock when wet. Because of its slippery nature, landslides can be common in areas where there is a lot of claystone in the ground.

sandstone

gritstone

mudstone

claystone

gritstone rocks in Peak District National Park in England

CHAPTER 5

LIFE SPAN OF SEDIMENTARY ROCKS

Just like all other rocks on Earth, sedimentary rocks do not last forever. All rocks are part of the rock cycle. Eventually, they will be recycled back into the ground and will turn into something else.

Earth has many naturally occurring cycles such as the water cycle, the nitrogen cycle, and the rock cycle. During the rock cycle, rocks are formed and then broken down. The pieces are formed into new rocks. For example, weathering can break down sedimentary rocks into new pieces of sediment. Those particles can then be moved by erosion and formed into another type of sedimentary rock.

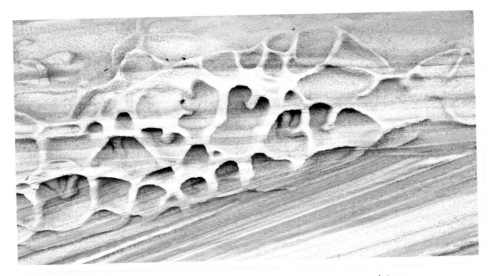

Weathering and erosion create unique shapes and patterns in sandstone found on the New South Wales coast.

Another example begins below Earth's crust where hot melted rock called magma is found. The magma rises to the surface through volcanic explosions. The magma that exits the crust is called lava. When lava cools, it becomes igneous rock. Over time, these rocks are broken down into sediments. They can be pressed together to form sedimentary rock. If enough heat and pressure are applied, it will turn into metamorphic rock. If the metamorphic rock is exposed to high enough heat, it will melt and turn back into magma. Then the rock cycle starts over again.

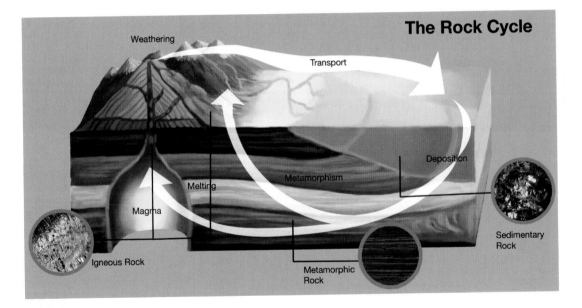

The Rock Cycle

Weathering
Transport
Deposition
Metamorphism
Melting
Magma
Igneous Rock
Metamorphic Rock
Sedimentary Rock

Tectonic plate movement drives the rock cycle. The plates move around on hot melted rock in Earth's mantle. The plates' movements have created mountains and other landforms. Weathering, erosion, and continued plate movement keep the rock cycle in motion.

cycle—a set of events that happens over and over again

tectonic plate—a gigantic slab of Earth's crust that moves around on magma

CHAPTER 6

USES OF SEDIMENTARY ROCKS

Sedimentary rocks are used for many purposes. One of the most common uses is building materials. Walls, roof tiles, and paving slabs can all be made out of sedimentary rocks.

Gypsum is sedimentary rock commonly used by builders. Gypsum is the powdery material found inside sheetrock, which is also known as drywall.

Limestone is sometimes crushed by machines and used to make concrete for roads and sidewalks. Powdered limestone is used in gardens to remove some of the acid from the soil. Limestone is used in the production of paper and in products that get rid of insects. Believe it or not, limestone is even used as the coating on certain types of chewing gum.

cement

drywall

Limestone has been used since ancient times. The pyramids of ancient Egypt were covered in a layer of limestone that gave them a crisp, white appearance. The stones were cut in such a way that the pyramids looked smooth. Today that limestone is nearly gone from the pyramids. Some of it was carted away to use on other projects. Some eroded due to weathering.

Clay is another sedimentary rock that has been in use for thousands of years. People in the Middle East were making clay bricks before 7500 BCE. They put water on the clay to make it soft. The muddy mixture was formed into bricks and put out in the sun to dry. When all of the water evaporated, the bricks became very hard. The bricks could then be used to build houses and other structures. Later, people put the bricks into large ovens to dry them. The hot temperatures made the bricks very strong. Fired bricks were used in ancient India and China as early as 3000 BCE.

Adobe bricks dry in the hot sun.

A power plant burns coal to produce energy.

Coal is another important sedimentary rock. Coal has been used for centuries for heating. The coal is burned, and the resulting heat boils water. The steam from the boiling water makes large turbines turn. The turbines cause a generator to produce electricity. In some places, coal is still used to heat homes. However, coal is not considered to be a "clean" fuel. Burning coal releases a lot of pollution into the air. Therefore, people now try to limit its use as much as possible.

GLOSSARY

breccia (BRECH-ee-uh)—sedimentary rock formed from jagged pieces of rock cemented together

conglomerate (kuhn-GLOM-er-it)—sedimentary rock formed from small, rounded chunks cemented together

crystal (KRIS-tuhl)—a solid substance having a regular pattern of many flat surfaces

cycle (SY-kuhl)—a set of events that happens over and over again

delta (DEL-tuh)—an area of land shaped like a triangle where a river enters a sea or ocean

erosion (i-ROH-zhuhn)—wearing away of rock or soil by wind, water, or ice

extract (ek-STRAKT)—to remove

fossil (FAH-suhl)—remains of an ancient plant or animal that have hardened into rock; also the preserved tracks or outline of an ancient organism

fossil fuel (FAH-suhl FYOOL)—natural fuel formed from the remains of plants and animals; coal, oil, and natural gas are fossil fuels

geologist (jee-AHL-uh-jist)—someone who studies minerals, rocks, and soil

reserve (ri-ZURV)—something stored or kept available for future use or need

stalactite (stuh-LAK-tyte)—a rock formation that hangs from the ceiling of a cave and is formed by dripping water

stalagmite (stuh-LAG-myte)—a rock formation that grows from the floor of a cave; it is formed when water drips onto the cave floor and leaves minerals behind

tectonic plate (tek-TON-ik PLAYT)—a gigantic slab of Earth's crust that moves around on magma

unique (yoo-NEEK)—one of a kind

weathering (WETH-er-ing)—breaking down of solid rock into smaller and smaller pieces by wind, water, glaciers, or plant roots

READ MORE

Nagle, Frances. *What Are Sedimentary Rocks?* A Look at Earth's Rocks. New York: Gareth Stevens Publishing, 2018.

Oxlade, Chris. *Minerals.* Rock On! Chicago: Heinemann Raintree, 2016.

Oxlade, Chris. *Rocks.* Rock On! Chicago: Heinemann Raintree, 2016.

Spilsbury, Richard. *Sedimentary Rocks.* Earth's Rocky Past. New York: PowerKids Press, 2016.

INTERNET SITES

Use FactHound to find Internet sites related to this book.

Visit *www.facthound.com*

Just type in 9781543527032 and go.

Check out projects, games and lots more at
www.capstonekids.com

CRITICAL THINKING QUESTIONS

1. What are two ways that sedimentary rocks can be broken apart and moved?

2. What are three uses for sedimentary rocks?

3. How are clastic rocks formed?

INDEX

31901063491189